HOCK AND SODA WATER

John Mortimer

HOCK AND SODA WATER

OBERON BOOKS
LONDON

First published in 2001 by Oberon Books Ltd.
(incorporating Absolute Classics)
521 Caledonian Road, London N7 9RH
Tel: 020 7607 3637 / Fax: 020 7607 3629
e-mail: oberon.books@btinternet.com
www.oberonbooks.com

Reprinted in 2003.

A catalogue record for this book is available from the British Library.

ISBN: 1 84002 258 2

Cover design: Andrzej Klimowski

Typography: Richard Doust

Printed in Great Britain by Antony Rowe Ltd, Chippenham.

I would to heaven that I were so much clay,
As I am blood, bone, marrow, passion, feeling –
Because at least the past were pass'd away –
And for the future – (but I write this reeling,
Having got drunk exceedingly today,
So that I seem to stand upon the ceiling)
I say – the future is a serious matter –
And so for God's sake – hock and soda water!

– Byron

Characters

HENRY TROUTBECK POTTINGER
as a Boy

HENRY TROUTBECK POTTINGER
as a Man

HENRY TROUTBECK POTTINGER
as an Old Man

DAWN POTTINGER
his Mother

THE REV. HENRY POTTINGER
his Father

MR REWCASTLE
a Dentist

FELICITY (FLISS or FLEA) REWCASTLE
his Daughter

MAVIS WHITNEY

EDITOR
of The Coldsands Sentinel

PHOTOGRAPHER

BARMAN

GIRL

The play takes place in and around the Vicarage of Coldsands-on-Sea. The set should be as simple as possible. There should be the suggestion of sea and of the arched window of the Vicarage or the Church. There needs to be a table and some chairs so the upstage area can become a bar, a dining room or an editor's office, etc. Various props can be brought on by the characters.

Hock and Soda Water was first performed at the Minerva Theatre, Chichester on 14 November 2001 with the following cast:

BOY (Henry), Sam Harding

MAN (Henry), Alan Cox

OLD MAN (Henry), Richard Johnson

DAWN POTTINGER, Dinah Stabb

REV. HENRY POTTINGER, Osmund Bullock

REWCASTLE/EDITOR, Peter Aubrey

FELICITY, Josephine Butler

MAVIS, Gemma Page

Other parts played by: Natasha Green and Ewan Watson

Director, Christopher Morahan

Designer, Deirdre Clancy

Lighting Designer, Wayne Dowdeswell

Musical Adviser, Gerry Berkley

Sound Designer, Tom Lishman

Choreographer, Terry John Bates

Costume Supervisor, Binnie Bowerman

ACT ONE

Darkness. The sound of wind and the sea. The stage lightens. The OLD MAN is standing watching. He stands in this way in silence for a while. Then he hears, off stage, the BOY shouting orders.

BOY: (*Off.*) Come on *mes braves!* Desert Scum! Beloved gaol birds! Heroes of the French Foreign Legion!
(*The BOY comes cantering on as though riding an imaginary horse.*)
To the battlements, you rogues and vagabonds! Prop the dead bodies of your fallen comrades in all the embrasures.

OLD MAN: What was the point of that, then?

BOY: To deceive the crafty Touaregs. The desert rebels on Arab steeds. They'll think we're four times the numbers.

OLD MAN: You're young now. You're too young to be defending Fort Zinderneuf with Beau Geste. You're only eleven...

BOY: I'm twelve!

OLD MAN: Not yet, are you?

BOY: Well, I'm twelve next birthday. I always tell people I'm twelve.

OLD MAN: Of course, you do. We have always specialised in small, unimportant lies. Why did you join the French Foreign Legion, by the way?

BOY: A stolen diamond.

OLD MAN: Of course!

BOY: My brother Beau was accused of stealing a diamond. We all went off to the Legion. Usually it's unhappy love affairs.

OLD MAN: At the age of eleven – what can you know about unhappy love affairs?

BOY: What do you know about them?

OLD MAN: I've had them. Naturally I've had them. And happy ones too. Which are considerably more painful.
(*Pause. The BOY, who has been answering naturally, now wonders.*)

BOY: Who are you anyway?

OLD MAN: Someone who's come to warn you.

BOY: Warn me of what?

OLD MAN: The time of your life will come. It will
  certainly come. When you'll hear a voice from the sky
  thundering. Perhaps the voice of God...thundering.

BOY: What?

OLD MAN: (*Loud and terrifying voice.*) From this day forth
  thou shalt not be able to put on thy socks!

BOY: (*Starting to laugh.*) That's ridiculous!

OLD MAN: Old age is, on the whole, a subject for ridicule.
  It will be your duty to leave the world as a sort of joke...

BOY: Anyway, I can put on my socks.

OLD MAN: And do up your laces?

BOY: Of course.

OLD MAN: Could you always...?

BOY: You mean the knots?

OLD MAN: I certainly mean the knots.

BOY: Perhaps. When I was first at nursery school. Miss
  Isabel helped me with the knots.

OLD MAN: I've got news for you.

BOY: Have you?

OLD MAN: You'll end up back in nursery school.

BOY: I don't think so.

OLD MAN: Of course you don't.

BOY: Anyway, I must go. Come on, *mes braves!* To the
  battlements!

OLD MAN: And you won't be able to fight Touaregs any
  more.

BOY: Why not?

OLD MAN: Politically incorrect.

BOY: What's that mean?

OLD MAN: You'll find out. Touaregs versus the French
  Foreign Legion? As some ethnic minority, the Touaregs
  would have to win.

BOY: Who can I fight then?

OLD MAN: Aliens. From Saturn. You can zap them with
  your space gun.

BOY: Can I zap Mamelukes?

OLD MAN: Afraid not… Anyway, you're not fighting anyone. You're not in command of the fort at Sidi Ben Abbas. You're a boy, somewhat short of inches. All alone in the garden of the Vicarage. Across the road from the Church of St. Stephen and All Angels. Son of the vicar, a priest of the Church of England, who has come to the reluctant conclusion that there's no one upstairs. A man who, having lost his faith in his profession, finds himself totally unqualified for any other job. So he carries on in the faint hope that God, if there is a God, might be bothered to grant him a revelation. You're in a garden full of dripping laurels, dying privet and gloomy rhododendrons. When I was your age, the garden seemed bigger than this.

BOY: It's enormous!

OLD MAN: Right next to the churchyard. Just over that wall. The graves.

BOY: I try not to look in that direction.

OLD MAN: So do I. (*Pause.*) More weeds than I remembered…

BOY: Weeds?

OLD MAN: Mutinying! Like the Mamelukes… Timbers, the jobbing gardener must be spending too much time trying to peer into the bedroom window…

BOY: What for?

OLD MAN: In the faint hope of seeing Mother take off her corsets.

BOY: My mother?

OLD MAN: Our mother.

BOY: (*Puzzled.*) Why would Timbers want to see her take off her corsets?

OLD MAN: Chronic uneventfulness of the private life. A complaint easily caught in the water-logged air of Coldsands-on-Sea.

BOY: Why did you tell me that?

OLD MAN: In the hope you might decide on…a change of climate.

BOY: I don't understand…

OLD MAN: Give yourself time. Not too much time, however. Then get out of it. Go! Look at me and you'll see what happens, in no time at all.

(*The light fades a little.*)

BOY: I can't see you. Where are you?

OLD MAN: It's getting dark.

BOY: Not really dark. Are you there?

OLD MAN: Here. In the garden.

BOY: I still can't see you.

OLD MAN: You will...

BOY: When?

OLD MAN: In approximately seventy years.

BOY: That's forever!

MOTHER: (*Calling crossly from off stage.*) Henry! Where are you?

BOY: Here I am.

OLD MAN: Why are you answering?

BOY: She sounds cross.

OLD MAN: I know. She calls us Harry when she's in a good mood. Hal when she's showing you off to friends. Henry when she's fed up to the teeth and remembers she's married to a man who prays regularly to nothing upstairs.

BOY: You're not Harry?

OLD MAN: Of course I am.

BOY: What're your other names?

OLD MAN: Henry Troutbeck Pottinger. What's yours?

BOY: Henry Troutbeck Pottinger. (*Pause.*) I don't know where the Troutbeck comes from.

OLD MAN: Mother's honeymoon in the Lake District. An isolated moment of delight in a small family hotel near Lake Windermere. That started it all.

BOY: What all?

OLD MAN: You and I. (*Pause.*) What did they call you at school?

BOY: Potty. What do they call you?

OLD MAN: Potty...Pottinger.

MOTHER: (*Calling, angry now, off stage.*) Hen...ree!

BOY: I'd better go in.

OLD MAN: Why?

BOY: It's getting dark.

OLD MAN: You'd better not.

BOY: Why ever...?

OLD MAN: Still light enough to run down to the beach. Where the sea breaks in white foam you can see by. Where you can strip off and feel the wet sand between your toes, oozing, and see the pimples on the beach where the razor fish will pop up if you drop salt on them. Leave your clothes in a bundle and swim away to a new life. They'll give you up for dead. With any luck.

MOTHER: (*Calling.*) Henry! Come at once! It's supper time!

BOY: You know what she's like. When supper's on the table...

OLD MAN: If only our mother had learnt to mash potatoes.

BOY: You mean...lumpy?

OLD MAN: And runny. A white gruel with pebbles you break your teeth on. Cabbage boiled into submission.

BOY: Wobbly jelly.

OLD MAN: Go on then. Make the best of it.

BOY: Shall I see you again?

OLD MAN: Inevitably.

(*The BOY moves upstage.*)

I've so little else to do.

(*Loud trumpeting sound as light comes up on upstage darkness. MOTHER and FATHER are now seated at the table having supper. The loud trumpeting sound is the VICAR blowing his nose. The BOY joins them at the table.*)

The Rev. Pottinger is clearing his passages. He has troubles with his sinuses.

(*A quieter trumpet by the FATHER.*)

Otherwise he sits mainly in silence. Trying to reconcile the existence of God with the problems of evil and blocked passages.

(*Pause.*)

MOTHER: More shepherd's pie, dear?

FATHER: Thank you, dear. That was ample.

(*The FATHER strikes his chest with his fist.*)

OLD MAN: Was that a sign of spiritual despair or indigestion?

FATHER: (*To MOTHER.*) I was talking to Arbuthnot after the Parish Council. His marriage is not a happy one. (*Pause.*) He tells me he and his wife plan to separate after the dog's passed over.

MOTHER: I suppose that's considerate of them.

FATHER: There seems so little respect for the institution of marriage in Coldsands nowadays. Oh yes. And I bumped into Rewcastle.

OLD MAN: Mr Rewcastle the dentist. A handsome man with soft brown eyes and dark curls. Looked as though he could have been a film star, but settled for a dental practice in Coldsands-on-Sea. When I heard the name I was filled with dread, hearing the buzz of his cumbersome drill, fearing his tentative probing at my misplaced teeth.

FATHER: I don't think he's a believer. But I don't love him any the less for that.

OLD MAN: He means he loves himself for tolerating the doubting dentist.

FATHER: I told him the breakdown of his marriage was a great sadness to us all.

MOTHER: Ssh, dear…

OLD MAN: Women fell in love with Mr Rewcastle. He sat them in the chair and he said, 'Just open wide for me now.' And they fell desperately in love.

FATHER: Apparently his wife just went off. Vanished. Not a word of warning.

MOTHER: *Pas avant,* dear.

FATHER: Left him with the child on his hands. I wouldn't give sixpence for her chances.

MOTHER: *Pas avant* the boy. Do you want some more shepherd's pie, Harry?

BOY: No thanks.

MOTHER: No thank you.

BOY: No thank you.

OLD MAN: No doubt it was a particularly nasty bit of shepherd.

(*Lights go down on the upstage area. Music off stage: 'You Are My Sunshine'.*

Downstage light comes up on a GIRL of about the boy's age. She is sitting holding a school book looking coolly at the upstage area.)

I remember the girl sitting on the dentist's stairs, looking down at the procession of patients with pity and contempt. Felicity, known to her friends as Fel Rewcastle, to her close friends as Flea or Fliss. The child of a broken home. With the chances our father wouldn't have given sixpence for. Apparently contented with her lot. Sitting on the stairs with black socks up to her pale, defenceless knees and a bang of her mother's chestnut hair. An expression of disillusioned amusement as she clutches the school book she's not reading.

(*Light upstage. The BOY in a chair. Mr REWCASTLE is approaching him with a buzzing drill.*)

REWCASTLE: Open wide for me...

BOY: (*His mouth wide open.*) I...M...O...enining...my

OLD MAN: Mr Rewcastle, the film star dentist, with his whirring drill, is approaching, almost apologetically, my open mouth innocent, as yet, of wisdom teeth.

REWCASTLE: (*Withdrawing the drill.*) Just rinse and spit for me will you?

OLD MAN: Why, I wondered, did Mr Rewcastle always ask people to rinse and spit for him... Couldn't he spit for himself? Does Flea say, 'What would you like for Christmas, Dad?' and he says, 'Just rinse and spit for me, darling'?

(*The BOY spits into a bowl.*)

REWCASTLE: Well done!

OLD MAN: Tell him it wasn't difficult.

(*The BOY says nothing.*)

REWCASTLE: Careful how you bite for a day or two. No toffee apples!

(*The BOY gets up, starts to go, looks towards FLEA.*)

BOY: Flea! I'm finished, Flea!

(*But FLEA gets up to go.*)

OLD MAN: But she has no time for you. She's vanishing into some cold privacy.

BOY: (*Calling after her.*) I was quite brave!

FLEA: (*With cold irony.*) You'll probably get a medal for it! (*She goes and the BOY goes.*
Sound of the sea is nearer. The BOY enters walking, his head down, looking for things on the beach. The OLD MAN is observing him.)

OLD MAN: Don't tell me. You've been marooned. Left on the pale shore of a desert island by the pirates who captured you...

BOY: The pirates I joined.

OLD MAN: Of course. I was forgetting.

BOY: Who marooned me after I quarrelled with their king.

OLD MAN: A quarrel... Over a woman?

BOY: Over the division of the treasure.

OLD MAN: Yes! That was it. So now you're searching the beach for...

BOY: Anything helpful...

OLD MAN: Driftwood to build a hut. A great chest, washed ashore in a sack. A case of brandy. Corn, to plant, so you can make your own bread... Have you found anything like that?

BOY: Not yet.

OLD MAN: And no sign of life on this island?

BOY: None!

OLD MAN: Not even a single footprint in the sand.
(*FLEA appears, her bathing suit wrapped in a towel under her arm. The BOY stops, and looks at her, his mouth open, amazed.*)

BOY: A fellow human being...!

FLEA: (*Cool.*) What are you talking about?

OLD MAN: And it speaks?

FLEA: Have you gone mad or what?

BOY: They told me... This island was completely uninhabited.

FLEA: (*Patient.*) It's the beach at Coldsands-on-Sea. Some people actually come here for their holidays. People who like a cold dip and sand in their ham rolls.

BOY: (*To FLEA.*) Now you're here you can help me.

FLEA: Help you do what?

BOY: Find driftwood. So I can build a hut.

FLEA: (*With contempt.*) You! Build a hut? Don't make me laugh.

BOY: Or just a handful of corn so I can grow bread.

FLEA: (*Still laughing.*) You can't even build card houses. Isn't it about time you grew up?

OLD MAN: She wants to get you off desert islands. And the search for treasure.

(*Pause.*)

FLEA: My father says they're going to give us another war…

BOY: Does he?

FLEA: You have to learn marching and how to stick bayonets into people. My father says a young officer only had a one in four chance of surviving more than two months in the last one.

BOY: I don't suppose I'll be a young officer.

FLEA: Then you'll be a tommy. It was a lot worse for tommies.

(*Pause.*)

BOY: (*Nervous.*) When's this war meant to start?

FLEA: Probably tomorrow. I'm going for a swim.

(*FLEA runs off with her towel and bathing suit. The BOY calls after her.*)

BOY: Flea!

OLD MAN: Flea never minded a cold dip.

(*The OLD MAN reappears upstage with the one-man band. There are drums, a triangle and a cymbal joined together in a sort of portable structure. This contraption is dusty, rusty in parts, but still playable.*)

The one-man-band. The junior drum set. We bought it with Aunt Queenie's Christmas money. And I found it in the loft last summer. Mildewed and partially eaten by mice.

(*The OLD MAN sings four lines from 'Night and Day' and beats the drums. The BOY enters. He joins in the beating of drums. The BOY sings the next five lines of 'Night and Day'.*)

They then sing the next three lines together; the OLD MAN sings two lines alone; they sing a line together.)

I almost forgot. You wanted to be Bing Crosby.

BOY: Fred Astaire.

OLD MAN: You can't dance…

BOY: What do you mean?

OLD MAN: Oh well… You'll find that out later. That song. I can remember all the words.

BOY: Not quite.

OLD MAN: I can't remember the words of the songs nowadays.

BOY: What's nowadays?

OLD MAN: Wherever you happen to be. Words have gone out of style. Shall we try it again?

(The OLD MAN and the BOY sing four lines from 'Night and Day'.)

And this…something won't be through.

BOY: Torment.

(The OLD MAN and the BOY sing the next four lines from 'Night and Day'. OLD MAN goes with one-man band. Light change. Light fades on the upstage area. The MOTHER is lit as she enters downstage with a bag of peas and a saucepan. She sits. Starts to shell the peas. The BOY joins her, helps with the shelling.)

BOY: Can I ask you something?

MOTHER: What's on the boy's mind now?

BOY: Have I got more than a one in four chance of staying alive?

MOTHER: *(Calmly shelling peas.)* Why? Are you feeling poorly?

BOY: Quite well thank you. *(Pause.)* It's the war.

(The OLD MAN comes into the downstage light. Watches the BOY and the MOTHER.)

Am I going to get killed in it…?

MOTHER: You mean are you going to die young?

OLD MAN: That's what you mean.

MOTHER: Your Uncle Harold did. And your Uncle Stanley. Uncle Stanley was hardly twenty… Your father's youngest brother.

BOY: Father didn't get killed.

MOTHER: No. He was a person with a sinus infection. That kept him out of it.

BOY: What killed them?

MOTHER: Some hopeless attack. Was it the same one? I can't remember – was it?

BOY: I don't know.

MOTHER: Anyway it was nothing they could help...

OLD MAN: She's hardly reassuring, is she? Our mother hasn't a great talent for setting minds at rest.
(*Pause.*)

BOY: I don't really want to die that young...

OLD MAN: Don't worry. You're not going to.

BOY: Not like Uncle Stanley...

OLD MAN: I said don't worry! You'll survive. I'm here to prove it to you. Can you hear me?

BOY: But I don't want to have to push bayonets into people. (*Pause.*) Is there really going to be a war?

OLD MAN: You'll certainly survive. It's the quality of the survival that might concern you.

MOTHER: War? I hardly think so.

BOY: Flea says there will be.

MOTHER: Flea?

BOY: Mr Rewcastle's daughter.

MOTHER: Poor child. I wouldn't give sixpence for her chances.

BOY: So isn't she right?

MOTHER: About what?

BOY: About the war?

MOTHER: (*Suddenly smiling. Her eyes brighter.*) I drove an ambulance in the last one.

BOY: You told me.

MOTHER: Not in the front line. Of course. Far enough away. But we could see the explosions. All the time. We heard the shelling. Our job was to take the wounded back to the hospitals. That's how I met your Uncle Harold. He said...'When you get back on leave why don't you meet my brother?' So I did. (*Pause. She sighs.*) And landed up in the Vicarage, Coldsands-on Sea. I don't think your father ever understood... It was terrible in France. Terrible. We saw so many wounded.

Horribly wounded. So many dead. And yet...those were days when I felt strangely happy. (*Pause.*) It's not going to happen again.

(*The MOTHER and the BOY go on shelling peas in silence.*)

BOY: Is that enough peas now?

MOTHER: Not quite yet... If a job is worth doing, it's worth doing properly.

(*Light change. Sound of the sea increases. FLEA runs upstage in her bathing suit. The BOY follows. He's undressing. Taking off his socks. The OLD MAN is watching.*)

BOY: (*To FLEA.*) My mother says the war's not going to happen.

FLEA: (*Ironic.*) Is your mother head of the government? (*She runs off. The BOY is pulling off his clothes, calls after her.*)

BOY: Wait for me.

OLD MAN: She's standing with white waves breaking at her knees. Felicity, Fliss, otherwise know as Flea rising from the sea. By the way, I admired the speed at which you took off your socks.

BOY: (*Calls.*) Wait! I'm coming!

OLD MAN: Two piles of clothes at the edge of the sea. Swim away and start a new life. Somewhere else. Everyone would take you for drowned.

BOY: (*Calls, anxious.*) Flea! (*Nervous but proud.*) She's swimming as though she'd swim forever...

OLD MAN: She won't go too far.

BOY: She might. She might do anything.

OLD MAN: Not quite...anything.

BOY: (*Calling against the sound of the sea.*) Flea! (*He runs off. Light fades to the sound of 'Smoke Gets in Your Eyes'. Then the trumpet of the FATHER clearing his sinuses. He appears in down stage light, wearing his surplice, preaching to his congregation (the audience).*)

FATHER: We live in anxious times. I expect you are all asking. Will there be a war – or will there, perhaps, not be a war? What does God want? He cannot, surely, be on the side of Nazi Germany. And yet he cannot, equally surely, want our young men slaughtered once again in the trenches. Has God still to make a choice, or has he, some of you may think, simply washed his hands of the whole business? Told us to 'Get on with it', to use a popular phrase. That our way of getting on with things means us killing each other. God, we say, exists because we believe in him. Does he exist because God believes in himself? In his infinite mercy, he may not tell us. He may keep us, for reasons best known to himself, in another popular phrase, 'in the dark'. He may, as the Government advertisements say, 'Be like Dad, Keep Mum.' Meanwhile, we can only tune into the news to learn what may, or may not, be his will.

OLD MAN: The congregation started to cough, sigh heavily and shuffle their feet. My father's sermons were not calculated to strengthen the sinews or summon up the blood.

FATHER: If you find these thoughts difficult to follow, perhaps we could proceed to something about which there can be no doubt or question. The excellence of the new kneelers so beautifully embroidered by Mrs Bulstrode and her loyal colleagues. Perhaps my favourite of all the kneelers is the one embroidered with the figure of a fisherman, perhaps reminding us of the apostle Peter, wearing a mackintosh and sou'wester hat. The typical image, if one may say it, of the inhabitants of Coldsands-on-Sea! So Lord, although your ways be mysterious, we give thanks to the talents and hard work of Mrs Bulstrode and her colleagues. And we dedicate their excellent kneelers to your service in the name of the Father, the Son and the Holy Ghost.

(*Light fades. The FATHER goes. Offstage song and music: 'We're Going to Hang out the Washing on the Siegfried Line.' We hear an air raid warning siren.*)

OLD MAN: During my school days a bomb fell on Coldsands pier. Another on a Wainscote haystack.

(*The BOY enters downstage, seems to be listening.*)

One night I came home from scouts and the Vicarage was, as I thought, empty. Then I heard a sound from the cupboard under the stairs, a place for keeping broken tennis racquets, wounded furniture, old telephone directories and a depleted croquet set. I took the sound for mice.

(*The BOY moves upstage where suddenly light reveals the MOTHER and FATHER as the OLD MAN describes them.*)

There were my father and mother, hand in hand, still as statues, waiting apparently for death.

FATHER: If you want to come into the cupboard, close the door after you.

(*The BOY moves away downstage as light fades on the FATHER and MOTHER.*)

OLD MAN: I didn't come in. I went into the garden.

(*The BOY looks upwards. Sound of distant bombs dropping.*)

I looked up at the sky and heard bombs drop far away. On other people.

(*The BOY goes. Leaving the OLD MAN alone on the stage. The sound of bombs dies away. The 'All Clear' siren goes. Then we hear offstage song and music: 'There'll be Blue Birds Over the White Cliffs of Dover.' As music fades the OLD MAN speaks.*)

Childhood ended and so did the war. I was born again, as an uncertain young man, driven by gusts of usually hopeless passion and in flight from often inevitable boredom.

(*The MAN enters, looks round, takes out a cigarette and a lighter, lights a cigarette.*)

I no longer commanded the Foreign Legion. I was a mocker of authority, who had never managed to be rude to a superior officer. A reader of Raymond Chandler who saw himself strolling down the mean streets of Coldsands-on-Sea smelling of Brylcreme and Capstan Full Strength. A would-be outsider who lived with his parents and carried, in his wallet, three French letters as beacons of hope.

(*The MAN looks in his wallet quickly and puts it away.*)

A demobilised young man looking for excitement in his life, at a hop in the village hall.

(*The MAN stamps out his cigarette as the music of 'Boomps-a-Daisy' starts. Offstage voices singing: 'Hands, Feet and Boomps-a-Daisy'. The MAN moves upstage where the light reveals FLEA grown up. She and the MAN start dancing together.*)

MAN: Flea.

FLEA: Oh, for God's sake, call me Felicity.

MAN: You dance beautifully.

OLD MAN: Damned silly thing to say…to anyone doing the Boomps-A-Daisy.

FLEA: Damn silly thing to say… You can't dance Boomps-A-Daisy beautifully!

OLD MAN: She appears cool as a cucumber. Don't let her fool you.

MAN: What did you say?

OLD MAN: I mean, you're a big boy now. Grown up and adult. Old enough to be hanged for murder. (*Pause.*) Don't try too hard…

(*Offstage the music changes, slows to 'I'll Be Seeing You/In All the Old Familiar Places'. The MAN and FLEA dance slowly together.*)

FLEA: So you're back from the army.

MAN: The Pay Corps in Cardiff.

FLEA: Doesn't sound very exciting.

MAN: Oh it was. So many girls… ATS, WRENS, WAAFS. You know what my old Sergeant used to say?

FLEA: How could I know?

MAN: There're two kinds of ATS. Felt 'ats and cocked 'ats. (*FLEA doesn't laugh.*)

FLEA: That's disgusting!

MAN: I know… That's exactly what I thought.

OLD MAN: Rubbish! You thought it was marvellously funny. (*Pause. They go on dancing.*)

FLEA: You're not going to boast to me are you? About the girls you once had.

MAN: No. Of course not.

OLD MAN: There weren't many were there?

MAN: Corporal Stella Jones in 'Marriage Allowances'.

OLD MAN: Was that all?

MAN: Others. Nearly…

(*Pause. The OLD MAN watches the dancing.*)

OLD MAN: We were never much of a dancer were we?

MAN: She likes my dancing…

OLD MAN: Just look at your feet. Clod-hopping. Determined to keep out of time with the music. I told you. We could never dance.

MAN: We? Who's 'we'?

OLD MAN: You and I. Have you given up dreams of becoming Fred Astaire?

MAN: I'm a journalist.

OLD MAN: Clattering away on the old Remington on the top floor of the Hotel Republica as the revolution reaches the square. Bullets bounce off the balcony and a beautiful native girl lies naked behind the mosquito nets…?

FLEA: What're you going to do now the war's over?

MAN: There's always a war somewhere…

FLEA: I suppose so.

MAN: Wherever it is, I'll be there. Clattering away on the old Remington on the top floor of the Hotel Republica with the revolution starting in the square.

(*The music stops. The MAN goes. FLEA applies her lipstick.*)

OLD MAN: She's thinking about your dream of a life in the front line of history. Deciding that it's probably time to wake you up…

(*The MAN returns with two glasses of beer. He hands one to FLEA, she drinks.*)

FLEA: I thought you worked on the Coldsands *Sentinel.*

OLD MAN: Got us there, hasn't she, my boy?

FLEA: I didn't know we had many revolutions. Flower shows, gymkhanas, happy couples showered with confetti and showing a full set of teeth. But very few revolutions…

OLD MAN: Try not to be turned on by the sharpness of her contempt. Don't try to win her over. You may go too far.

MAN: The *Sentinel's* only a temporary job. I'm on my way to Fleet Street.

FLEA: And then…?

MAN: Mexico…Chile…Malaya…Wherever there's trouble.

FLEA: You believe that?

OLD MAN: Well. You should have faith. Our father was less gloomy when he believed there was someone listening when he knelt in prayer.

MAN: Of course. Do you think I'm going to spend my life here? Shall we dance again…?

FLEA: If you want to.

(*The MAN and FLEA dance to the 'Tennessee Waltz'.*)

OLD MAN: May I just remind you of what's to come?

MAN: No thanks.

FLEA: What did you say?

MAN: Nothing. I said nothing…

OLD MAN: It's not only that you won't be able to dance. You'll have to plan standing up. Take a deep breath. Count to three. And heave yourself up by the arms of the chair. Have you ever considered how you're going to get out of the bath?

MAN: Oh, do be quiet!

FLEA: I didn't say anything.

OLD MAN: You'll have flopped into the soapy water somehow, producing a tidal wave. Slide one ailing leg over the side and lever yourself up, shoulders sliding up the wall. Get the edge of the bath between your buttocks and heave. Splash down again if you're not successful. You'd have less trouble rising from the dead…

MAN: Your future! Not mine…

(*He and FLEA dance off. The music changes to a brass band, playing cheerfully. In sunlight upstage, the table is covered with flowers, fruit and vegetables. The MAN enters with a notebook. Looks at the produce on the table, makes a note.*)

OLD MAN: The fete in the Vicarage garden. Cucumbers with elephantiasis. Portly onions, plumped up marrows. Obese potatoes, long and lanky broad beans, mammoth tomatoes, shiny as boils, or skin eruptions. Wearing the badges of first, second or third prize, like long service medals at regimental dinners. A hot afternoon organised by the Church wardens for the steeple restoration fund.

(*The MAN is looking at an exhibit – a farm workers lunch.*
MAVIS enters, speaks to the MAN.)

MAVIS: Are you taking an interest in the farm worker's
lunch?

OLD MAN: The girl who spoke had colourless hair and
eyelashes that disappeared in the sunlight. She talked
breathlessly as though she had just bicycled up a long hill.

MAVIS: It's jolly good actually.

OLD MAN: There was a Cornish pasty, an apple, a piece of
cake and a bottle with a screw top…

MAN: Cider?

MAVIS: It's not cider, it's apple juice. My mother thought a
whiff of cider would have them dropping off the tractor,
or scything their legs off, most likely.

MAN: Is this yours. This exhibit?

MAVIS: It's all home-made, in fact. The Cornish pasty and
the Dundee cake also. No, it's not mine. My mother's.
She goes in for that sort of thing. I'm Mavis Whitney, by
the way. She's Mrs Whitney.

(*The MAN makes a note.*)

OLD MAN: She has small, white teeth, which look sharp as
razors. She smiles all the time. Do you know what she's
smiling at?

MAN: I imagine she's just being polite.

OLD MAN: You imagine wrong.

MAN: I wrote her name in my spiral notebook.

OLD MAN: With no intention of using it in your piece.
'Mavis' mother's farm worker's lunch wins second prize
in church fete'. Hardly a banner headline.

MAVIS: Mum will be so thrilled. Everyone reads the *Sentinel.*

MAN: I'll do my best to get your mother in.

MAVIS: Oh, squeeze her in. Do!

OLD MAN: I move. Closing the spiral notebook.

MAVIS: Do farm workers really carry their food about in
handkerchiefs any more?

MAN: (*Further away.*) I don't answer her.

OLD MAN: Why not?

MAN: I think it a rather silly remark. From a girl with
invisible eyelashes.

MAVIS: Whitney. W.H.I.T.N.E.Y. Goodbye for now. (*She goes.*)

OLD MAN: It doesn't occur to you…?

MAN: What?

OLD MAN: She was taking the mick.

MAN: Out of me?

OLD MAN: All too easy a thing to do.

MAN: What do you mean?

OLD MAN: In time you'll discover.

> (*The MAN has gone upstage. Downstage, a table, on it an old fashioned typewriter and sheets of copy. At it is the EDITOR of the* Sentinel *in his short sleeves with braces and sleeve bands. He is looking at a letter with particular distaste.*)
> The Editor of the *Sentinel.* Sam Brackett. Bracelets on his shirt sleeves because he'd seen an editor wearing those in a film in the Coldsands Odeon.
> (*There's a knock. The MAN enters.*)

EDITOR: Pottinger! Come in.

MAN: You wanted to see me, sir?

OLD MAN: Very polite. Hardly any mocking of authority today.

EDITOR: This woman sent in a poem. She says you encouraged her…

MAN: Which woman is that, sir?

EDITOR: Calls herself Mavis Whitney.

MAN: Oh, that woman.

EDITOR: (*Handing the letter to the MAN.*) Just read it, would you? Just cast your eye over it. I want your impression. (*Pause.*) Well. What do you think?

MAN: It rhymes…

EDITOR: The subject matter, Pottinger! I wasn't asking about the rhymes. They seem to be adequate, even skilful. What's your impression of the subject matter? (*Pause.*)

MAN: Unusual.

EDITOR: To put it mildly.

MAN: Very unusual, sir.

EDITOR: I take it it's not a usual practise, among the female population of Coldsands, to smear their bodies with honey?

MAN: I wouldn't know about that, sir.

EDITOR: It would require pots of the stuff to cover some of our lady readers.

MAN: I can see that.

EDITOR: And can you see what she suggests in the last verse?

MAN: The last verse, sir?

EDITOR: She seems to be calling on some unnamed male to lick it off her.

MAN: I noticed that.

EDITOR: So did I. In fact, if you read the damn thing, you can't help noticing it. This poem is muck, Pottinger. It's the only word I can find adequate.

MAN: Yes, sir.

EDITOR: We pride ourselves on high standards here at the *Sentinel*, Pottinger. I myself have the highest standards in matters sexual. You may call me old fashioned, but no woman shall ever touch my underclothes...
(*Pause.*)

MAN: What would you like me to do with this poem, sir?

EDITOR: Bin it! File it in the WPB... Better still, burn it. Advise this Whitney woman that we don't print pornographic muck in the Coldsands *Sentinel*. Understand?

OLD MAN: Did you tell him to print the poem? In full. To wake up the neighbourhood. To startle them into interesting variations on the act of love.

MAN: I understand, sir.

OLD MAN: You did not.
(*The MAN starts to go.*)

EDITOR: Oh and Pottinger...

MAN: (*Stops.*) Yes, sir?

EDITOR: I'm going to send you on a mission. We want a full report of an event. Go on Saturday...

MAN: (*Hopeful.*) Is it abroad, sir?

EDITOR: Not quite. Just all the way to Wilmington-on-Sea. There's a posh wedding in the Benbow family. Describe the scene. Soak up the atmosphere. I can let you have... well – a good half column. Mix with the guests. You'll enjoy that, won't you?

MAN: (*Rueful.*) I suppose... I'll quite enjoy it, Mr Bracket. (*Sound of an organ playing 'Here Comes the Bride'. A wedding is going on in an offstage church, from which the happy couple are emerging, also offstage. A PHOTOGRAPHER runs across with a camera on a tripod. MAVIS approaches and throws a handful of confetti in the offstage direction. The MAN enters with his notebook, late and writing hastily. MAVIS looks at him.*)

MAVIS: Still working for the *Sentinel?*

MAN: I'm afraid so.

MAVIS: Did your editor like my poem?

MAN: I have to say, he was profoundly shocked.

MAVIS: You weren't?

MAN: Of course not!

OLD MAN: Don't tell her that you agreed with your editor.

MAVIS: Shocking the dear old *Sentinel.* It's too easy isn't it?

MAN: Well. It's not hard.

MAVIS: You ought to get out of it. Work for a national.

MAN: (*Casual.*) Oh, I mean to.

MAVIS: Let me tell you. What you need is a scoop. Not just for the 'Sentinel'. If your Editor got a scoop he wouldn't know what to do with it... Get a story that'll be picked up by Fleet Street.

MAN: Is Fleet Street going to be interested in the Benbow wedding...?

MAVIS: It might be... (*Thoughtful.*) It might just possibly be. (*The PHOTOGRAPHER comes back across the stage with his camera and tripod.*)

PHOTOGRAPHER: (*Calls out as he passes.*) They don't want any photographs.

MAVIS: Interesting...

MAN: Is it?

MAVIS: Interesting that they don't want any photographs...

MAN: Why?

MAVIS: Photographs might give the game away...

MAN: What game?

MAVIS: You mean you don't know.

MAN: Know about what?

MAVIS: The wedding.

MAN: Tell me…

MAVIS: Well. Charlie Benbow had an uncle in South America. He never saw much of the family. But he left an absolute fortune to Charlie provided he married Dolly Fairweather. It seems the uncle had met her and took a huge shine.

MAN: (*Who has been taking notes.*) So he did marry her. Today.

MAVIS: No! That's the whole point. Dolly refused point blank and went off to live with some hugely dull chap in the Australian outback. She's disappeared entirely from view.

MAN: So who was that in the church…going up the aisle?

MAVIS: This is where it gets interesting… You know Dolly was a twin. The other…

MAN: Identical?

MAVIS: Very similar. Except he was a boy.

MAN: So you're not telling me…?

MAVIS: A veil, a wig and bit of make up. The wedding dress hid the rest of it. I thought Tommy Fairweather made a beautiful bride…

MAN: What's going to happen now?

MAVIS: Charlie Benbow will toddle off to South America and pick up the uncle's swag. Tommy's looking for a career in the army!

(*The MAN looks at her, then laughs.*)

MAN: That's the most wildly improbable story.

OLD MAN: Those are always the best ones to believe in.

MAVIS: You'd like it confirmed. By a reliable witness?

MAN: That's impossible!

MAVIS: I don't know. There's Tommy's girlfriend. She's sick as a parrot about the whole business.

MAN: I suppose she would be…

MAVIS: I'll see if I can get her to talk to you.

MAN: Don't go to any trouble.

MAVIS: Oh I have to.

MAN: Why?

MAVIS: Because if I don't your piece in the *Sentinel*'s going to be extremely dull… (*Pause.*) You know where I live in Coldsands?

MAN: I don't actually.

MAVIS: Down by the bus station. You could come down there. If you wanted to be a bit sordid.

MAN: Why? Is it sordid by the bus station?

OLD MAN: Sometimes I despair of you! Just go. Go down to the bus station – find out what she means by *sordid*. (*The MAN starts to go.*)

MAVIS: (*Looks at him. Regretful smile.*) Where are you going?

MAN: Back to work I suppose. As there's no story yet.

OLD MAN: Of course there's a story! It's just that you didn't understand it.

(*Light fades downstage. Upstage light. Hall in the Vicarage, only indicated by a telephone on a small stool. The MAN moves upstage, his MOTHER and FATHER are standing watching him as he moves to go. The OLD MAN is also there.*)

MOTHER: Where are you going?

MAN: Just...out.

MOTHER: Where are you going out?

MAN: (*Sighs.*) Mother. Do you have to know?

OLD MAN: She has to.

MAN: To meet a friend.

MOTHER: Not that Rewcastle girl?

MAN: Yes. That girl, if you have to know.

FATHER: I think what troubles your mother...

OLD MAN: A worried word from the doubting vicar.

FATHER: ...is that her family life has hardly brought her up with a respect for marriage...

OLD MAN: Did they respect it, we wonder? Those long evenings with nothing to say to each other. Perhaps they did. It was a sort of abstract respect. In the way people respected the Royal Family, or the police if they'd never been arrested.

(*The telephone rings.*)

FATHER: That's the telephone.

OLD MAN: It was the one thing the vicar could be certain of. (*MAVIS appears downstage, holding a telephone.*)

MAN: Hallo...

MOTHER: Is it that girl?

MAVIS: It's Mavis Whitney. I might get Tommy's girlfriend to talk. Can we meet?

MAN: When?

MAVIS: Preferably tonight.

MAN: I'm afraid I'm busy tonight.

MAVIS: What're you so busy about?

MAN: Working. It's the *Sentinel.*

MAVIS: Is there an epidemic of Women's Institute meetings? Or an exceptional turnover in births and deaths?

MAN: Afraid so…

MAVIS: All right then. Some other time. I'm sorry about tonight. It could've been fun.

(*MAVIS moves away.*)

OLD MAN: You never understood how much she fancied us. Well, you, not me…

(*Lights fade upstage. Offstage song and music: 'Walking my Baby Back Home'.*

Light upstage. A bar. FLEA and the MAN are together drinking beer in a Coldsands pub. Pub noises.)

FLEA: Your mother doesn't approve of me.

MAN: It's not that…

FLEA: Your family doesn't approve at all. It's because I'm the child of a broken home.

MAN: I rather envy you…

FLEA: What?

MAN: I often wish my home would break up. They sit there in silence, with nothing at all to say to each other. Will you have another beer?

FLEA: I'm all right, thanks.

MAN: Of course you're all right. But will you have another Symington's?

FLEA: If you're asking me.

MAN: I am.

FLEA: Then, no. (*Pause.*) I believe marriage is for life.

OLD MAN: Startling, wasn't it. From wild Felicity. From reckless Felicity, who goes on swimming, pale and naked, much too far out into the cold sea.

FLEA: I'm sure your parents believe that it's for life.

MAN: On most subjects my father is in a state of perpetual doubt.

FLEA: I went to see my mother. She's living with a chiropodist in Croydon.

OLD MAN: She means, 'Bit of a comedown from a dental surgeon.'

FLEA: All sorts of people come to the house and offer my mother's lover their feet. (*Pause.*) He's got my father's eyes, but not nearly so well set. He drinks much more than my father. He belches after supper and says, 'Pardon me.' When she makes a suggestion he says, 'Don't trouble your pretty head, Eileen. I'll take it on my own broad shoulders.' I bet she wishes her first marriage had been for life.

(*Pause. A BARMAN appears.*)

MAN: You really don't want another Symington's?

FLEA: You don't, do you?

MAN: I just might. Well, just a half... Just one half of Symington's, Bob. Are you sure you won't?

FLEA: (*Looking offstage.*) Who's that?

MAN: What?

FLEA: Who's that looking at you? With sandy hair and no eyebrows.

MAN: (*Looks, answers in a casual manner.*) Oh, that. It's Mavis.

FLEA: Mavis Whitney? Of course. She was at school. In the year below. She didn't stand out much, which is why I couldn't remember. Same colour as the beige walls. She was sort of camouflaged. Look out. She's coming this way...

(*MAVIS enters.*)

MAVIS: Oh, hullo. Working hard tonight, are you?

MAN: (*Embarrassed.*) Hullo, Mavis.

MAVIS: Flea! We were at school together...

FLEA: I think we were. Now you remind me. Not everyone calls me Flea, by the way. To most people I'm Felicity.

MAVIS: You were always Flea at school, so far as I remember. (*To the MAN.*) So. Flea's your hard work, is she?

MAN: We're just having a drink together.

MAVIS: Just? How disappointing.

(*The MAN looks offstage.*)

BARMAN: Here's your other half.

MAN: Thank you, Bob…

FLEA: (*Looking offstage.*) Weren't you with those people?

OLD MAN: The group Mavis has just left. Older men. One smoking a pipe.

MAVIS: Fellows.

OLD MAN: Older women with dark hair flattened down like seals, deep, soft voices and fishermen's sweaters.

FLEA: Is that what you call them?

OLD MAN: A single call chap with a blonde lock of falling hair and a prominent Adam's apple.

MAVIS: I mean Dons. Teachers. So called experts in their particular fields. The one with a long neck thinks he taught me English. Bit of a twerp actually.

OLD MAN: They were all looking across at Mavis as though they missed her company.

FLEA: I wouldn't know. I never went to university.

MAVIS: Lucky escape. You missed Hector Glasscock.

MAN: Is that his name?

MAVIS: Not quite. We call him that. Glasstock, actually. Only two books he's ever read are *Lord of the Flies* and *1984.* Oh, and he's mad about the Hobbits. Absolutely hopeless on Byron.

OLD MAN: The tall one is now drinking to Mavis. Raising his glass and quaffing his beer.

FLEA: I'm rather like the Hobbits.

MAVIS: Boring little creatures with fur between their toes. I can't stand them.

MAN: Can I buy you a drink, Mavis?

MAVIS: 'I would to heaven that I were so much clay,
As I am blood, bone, marrow, passion, feeling –
Because at least the past were pass'd away –
And for the future – (but I write this reeling,
Having got drunk exceedingly today,
So that I seem to stand upon the ceiling)
I say – the future is a serious matter –
And so – for God's sake – hock and soda water!'
It'll be white plonk here, though.

MAN: (*To the BARMAN.*) White wine and soda.

BARMAN: (*To MAVIS.*) Who wrote that?

MAVIS: Him.

FLEA: Him with the long neck?

MAVIS: No, him. Lord Byron.

MAN: I haven't read very much...

MAVIS: Oh you should... What a man!

OLD MAN: Bad, mad and dangerous to know...

MAVIS: I like him best in Venice.

MAN: Venice?

MAVIS: The palace on the grand canal. Filled with pets, birds, dogs and monkeys. Seductions in his gondola and then back to his furious mistress the housekeeper or the little Baccante in bed upstairs.

MAN: (*Appreciative.*) That was the life!

MAVIS: At least, it gave him plenty to write about.

FLEA: Is that all that matters?

MAVIS: You don't think so...?

FLEA: I don't suppose the house keeper thought that poetry was any sort of excuse for the girl upstairs.

MAVIS: Probably not.

FLEA: But then I don't suppose she read much of his poetry, do you? I always thought Byron was a bit of a sham. Pretending to be so romantic and...

MAVIS: But he was funny. Really funny.

(*The BARMAN appears with MAVIS's drink.*)

MAN: Is that enough soda water?

MAVIS: Fine.

(*She knocks it back in one huge gulp. The MAN watches her with admiration; FLEA with disgust. MAVIS looks at them both, smiles.*)

I'd better get back to my academics...

(*She goes upstage. FLEA watches her go.*)

FLEA: If I had those invisible eyelashes at least I'd colour them up a little. (*Pause.*) She's got a cheek.

MAN: What?

FLEA: I said 'she's got a cheek'. Coming over to us and talking all that nonsense about Byron.

MAN: I don't think it was nonsense.

FLEA: Oh really? I suppose that's what you'd've liked to have been wouldn't you? Having it off with cheap girls in gondolas and keeping apes.

MAN: Not a bad sort of life when you come to think of it.

FLEA: I suppose that's what you wanted to be wasn't it?

MAN: What?

(*MAVIS appears upstage, watches the quarrel.*)

FLEA: The Don Juan of the Pay Corps. Getting inside all them women's army regulation knickers and boasting about it to anyone who's got the patience to listen! (*She starts to go.*) I'm not enjoying this pub any more.

MAN: Flea...

(*She goes. He starts after her.*)

FLEA: Thanks. I can find my own way home. Why don't you phone for a gondola?

(*As she goes MAVIS watches her. The MAN, left alone, finishes his drink.*

Lights fade on the upstage area. Then the MAN appears downstage. The OLD MAN watches him.)

OLD MAN: The way home to the vicarage was down Mafeking Street, past Copenhagen Crescent and then came to a dark road past the graves. When we were a boy, our bedroom looked out over the churchyard. Each morning I saw pale light on white granite crosses, wilting chrysanthemums on marble slabs. I always thought I heard...

MAN: Fingers scrabbling, fists beating on coffins. The not quite dead screaming to get out.

OLD MAN: Or the entirely dead...

MAN: All the sounds quiet, of course, and muffled. Small and helpless underground disturbances.

OLD MAN: Merely murmurs.

(*MAVIS enters in upstage darkness.*)

MAVIS: You've got here at last...

MAN: Who...?

MAVIS: You know perfectly well. It's Mavis Whitney. I've been waiting for you.

MAN: Why on earth?

MAVIS: Why don't you come and see. (*Pause.*) You're not frightened of walking through the churchyard are you?

OLD MAN: Be honest. Say 'yes'.

MAN: No. Of course I'm not frightened. I used to play here when I was a child.

OLD MAN: Complete lies. I think she wants you to stop talking.

(*Light upstage. We see MAVIS standing by a grave stone. Her shirt is open to the waist. She moves towards the MAN.*)

MAN: I agreed with a lot of what you said about Byron.

MAVIS: Just be quiet.

(*MAVIS stands in front of the MAN, her hands go to his flies. She doesn't kiss him.*)

OLD MAN: Her fingers are unbuttoning your fly as delicately as her mother had taught her to hold a tea cup. Was it buttons, in those days?

MAN: An early zip.

(*Now MAVIS kisses him. The MAN returns the kiss passionately. They sink down beside the grave stone. They are making love.*)

OLD MAN: Lying together on a green mound, softer than the vicarage beds. 'Ethel Bembridge, widow, late of this parish'. You can see the light in your father's study as he wrestles to complete a sermon without any embarrassing reference to the Almighty. Now, his light's gone out... And, it seem, you've lost your fear of churchyards.

(*Light goes down on the upstage area. The MAN and MAVIS get up and go.*)

When it was over we rose like ghosts from the grave.

(*The MAN and MAVIS enter downstage, hand in hand. They stand facing each other before parting.*)

MAN: I'll see you back home.

MAVIS: Don't bother. I know the way.

MAN: So tomorrow...

MAVIS: What about tomorrow?

MAN: Perhaps I'll see you.

MAVIS: Perhaps.

OLD MAN: Don't let it be 'perhaps'. Don't let it! Go with her! Go now. Her home's by the bus station... Don't lose her.

MAVIS: Sleep well.

MAN: Sleep well.

(*They kiss and leave in opposite directions. Light change. The MAN moves downstage.*)

She went then. She went forever.

OLD MAN: Why did you let her go?

MAN: I only left it for a couple of days.

OLD MAN: Too long...

MAN: Flea made up our quarrel.

OLD MAN: That was the trouble.

MAN: She said she really wanted to have supper with my parents.

OLD MAN: That should've been a terrible warning.

MAN: I found out Mavis had left her room.

OLD MAN: Down by the bus station...

MAN: I saw her teachers again in the pub.

OLD MAN: She walked out on the University.

MAN: No one knew where she walked to.

OLD MAN: You could've found out. If you'd really wanted to. You could've found out.

(*The MAN opens his wallet, looks in it, dismayed and anxious for a moment. Then shrugs and pulls out a piece of paper.*)

MAN: Mavis's sent me another poem.

OLD MAN: Not by her, however.

MAN: (*Reading.*) 'For the sword outwears its sheath,
  And the soul wears out the breast,
  And the heart must pause to breathe,
  And love itself have rest.'
  I like that poem.

OLD MAN: It started us reading Byron. Our first glimpse into another world. (*Pause.*) Byron, and Mavis of course.

MAN: She sent me that and vanished. I never saw her again.

OLD MAN: I did.

MAN: When?

(*Pause. The OLD MAN looks at him.*)

OLD MAN: You'll have to wait and see.

End of Act One.

ACT TWO

Light downstage. The OLD MAN enters.

OLD MAN: Where were we exactly? Of course. I remember.
  We'd been in the graveyard. A place once to be avoided.
  Now never to be forgotten. Mavis had gone… Flea was
  back…with a strange desire to share in Shepherd's Pie at
  the Vicarage.
  (*Light upstage. Supper at the Vicarage. FATHER, MOTHER,
  MAN, FLEA at supper. The OLD MAN is watching.*)

FLEA: That was absolutely delicious.

MOTHER: It's only shepherd's pie…

FLEA: Mmmm…

MOTHER: Do have seconds…

MAN: You don't have to.

FLEA: Oh, but I want to. I really want to.
  (*The MOTHER refills FLEA's plate.*)

OLD MAN: Why weren't those words a sort of warning?

MAN: She was only being polite.

OLD MAN: I think, she has other things in mind.

MOTHER: How is your father…?

FLEA: Oh, you know, working hard…

OLD MAN: Thanks to the great popularity of boiled sweets
  among the citizens of Coldsands.

FATHER: We have a great admiration for your father.

OLD MAN: For his bridge work?

FATHER: For carrying on. In such difficult circumstances.

FLEA: (*Solemn.*) I think it's his faith that keeps him going.

OLD MAN: Can you believe what you're hearing?

MAN: No. Quite honestly.

FATHER: Your father has it? (*Pause.*) Your father has faith?

OLD MAN: The note in our father's voice was pure envy.

FLEA: Oh yes. Always.
  (*Pause.*)

MOTHER: We don't see him in church very often…

OLD MAN: So like Mother. To put a spanner in the works.

39

FLEA: (*Still solemn.*) I wouldn't say he's one for the formalities. I think he finds his religion in his life, and in his work.

OLD MAN: Drilling a tooth for Jesus.

FATHER: We don't love him any the less for not coming to church.

OLD MAN: Our father talked about love the whole time. It came into all his sermons, cropping up in vast quantities on Sunday mornings. He spread it around his parish on the good and evil, the beautiful and ugly, the kindly and the bloody minded, spraying it on evenly, like some sort of insecticide. And then the tin was empty. There seemed to be very little left for him. Do you think he and Mother...?

MAN: Please! I don't want to think about it.

OLD MAN: What do you want to think about?

(*Pause. The MAN doesn't answer.*)

I know. I know exactly. You're remembering.

MAN: Remembering what?

OLD MAN: The distant sound of the sea. The mound of grass as soft as a mattress.

MAN: The graveyard...

OLD MAN: Exactly. Now it's become a place – to remember with delight.

MAN: (*Smiles.*) Ethel Bembridge. Late of this Parish. Her grave and Mavis so alive. She's gone. Mavis has gone...

OLD MAN: Go after her!

MAN: Where? I don't know where.

OLD MAN: Find out... Don't just sit there. Find out.

MAN: I'd better give up. Thinking about Mavis.

OLD MAN: Don't ever. Don't ever give up.

(*They finished eating. FLEA stands, starts to pile the plates.*)

Can't you see? Something rather disturbing is taking place.

MAN: What exactly?

OLD MAN: Flea. She's going to help with the washing up.

MOTHER: There's no need for you to do that...

FLEA: It's absolutely no trouble.

MOTHER: I can cope quite easily.

FLEA: Why don't I wash and you dry? Is that a fair division of labour?

(*FLEA goes out with the plates. The MOTHER follows her.*)

FATHER: Rewcastle has faith.

MAN: So Flea said.

FATHER: A man whose wife left him. Who spends his days gazing down people's mouths, searching for rotten teeth! Can still find faith in God?

MAN: So it seems.

FATHER: There is a lesson there for all of us.

(*Sound of the sea as light fades upstage.*
Downstage, in light, the MAN and his MOTHER are walking.
The OLD MAN is watching.)

MAN: My mother suggested, unusually, a walk along the beach...

OLD MAN: Where a cold wind flicked at the waves and wet dogs capered and urinated in the surf. Lifting their legs and turning the yellow foam yellower.

MOTHER: Felicity seems a very suitable sort of girl...

OLD MAN: Suitable! Did you want to hear Flea called suitable?

MAN: I have to say it surprised me. As though she were curtain material that 'went with' the sitting room carpet. 'Suitable'.

OLD MAN: But you don't agree with the description.

MAN: Except to ask... (*Pause.*) Suitable for what, Mother?

MOTHER: Oh, just generally suitable. I had nothing particularly in mind. But now you're Deputy Editor...

OLD MAN: Deputy Editor of the Coldsands *Sentinel*. Now there's a step up the ladder of fame.

MOTHER: Well. We've got to think of the future, haven't we? (*She goes.*)

OLD MAN: Holding out your sock like a limp net with a white foot wandering towards it. Arms stretched but not far enough to catch the tremulous toes. Stoop to pick up a dropped envelope and the blood tumbles to your head, you stagger like a stunned boxer. That's the future, if we have to be honest.

MAN: There's no point in telling me that.

OLD MAN: No point at all.

MAN: I don't believe it, for a start.

OLD MAN: Of course you don't.

MAN: I don't consider the putting on of the socks as a great test of endurance.

OLD MAN: Not like marriage, for instance.

MAN: That didn't seem a particularly difficult thing, either.

OLD MAN: Not an athletic feat, you mean?

MAN: It all seemed to happen...well, almost all...like a dream.

OLD MAN: You awoke and found yourself married.

(*Light upstage. The MAN, FLEA and the VICAR.*)

FATHER: Are you sure you're ready for marriage?

MAN: Not at all sure.

FATHER: I don't really suppose one ever is. Perhaps it's something that steals up on you. Like faith. Or influenza. Of course, your mother and I have been very happy. But I think of Jesus...

MAN: I suppose you have to...

FATHER: He had very little time for family life. Left home early. Never married at all. Said, 'who is this woman?' to his mother. Of course, he had faith. Faith is a great thing to have.

MAN: So I believe.

FATHER: (*To FLEA.*) I shall, of course, be marrying you myself.

FLEA: (*Surprised.*) Really?

FATHER: I mean, I shall be conducting the ceremony. What did you think I meant?

MAN: Wouldn't that be a little incestuous?

FATHER: It will be...entirely appropriate. As, of course, I know you so well...

OLD MAN: Do you, I wonder. Do you really know us at all?

FATHER: I shall not need to give you the usual instruction on marriage.

FLEA: Oh please do! As we're getting married, we want the whole shooting match. All the trimmings. If it wasn't us, what would you say?

FATHER: I'd say marriage may seem all very fine and large to you now. I'd say that to the young couple, when the wife is fresh and shapely and the husband virile, marriage may seem something to be looked forward to like a summer holiday. But you know, that young woman is going to lose her looks. She'll put on middle aged spread and gasp going upstairs... That young man will have, let us say, back problems and be passed over for promotion. Then, I say to my young couples, you will see what marriage is really all about.

FLEA: What is it about then?

FATHER: A test. A test of endurance. Like climbing Everest. Or walking to the South Pole. A challenge from which you can emerge triumphant.

FLEA: And you and his mother emerged triumphant?

FATHER: In our own small way. I think we did.

OLD MAN: He means they climbed a small hill, or got as far south as Bognor.

FATHER: Have you settled on anywhere for the honeymoon...? In the view of your mother and myself, you can't do better than the Lake District...

MAN: We were thinking about Venice...

FLEA: Oh no. Not Venice. I've always wanted to see the Lake District.

(*Light fades upstage. The OLD MAN is lit downstage.*)

OLD MAN: The honeymoon. 'Treacle Moon,' Lord Byron called it. But first the marriage. A strange experience. My father standing there in his full canonicals, uniting us for the foreseeable future. What did Lord B say of a similar occasion?

'And he stood calm and quiet, and he spoke
The fitting vows, but heard not his own words,
And all things reeled about him; he could see
Not that which was, but that which should have been...'

After that the reception. A tent was put up in the vicarage garden. Champagne was available, all paid for by Mr Rewcastle.

(*The MAN enters with a glass of champagne. He is followed by REWCASTLE, also with a glass of champagne.*)

43

REWCASTLE: She'll stick to you, you know. You needn't worry about that.

MAN: I don't worry.

REWCASTLE: She's determined to show her mother how to stick to a marriage. How to be incredibly loyal.

MAN: Well, that's good...

REWCASTLE: If you think so. Her mother bunked off you know.

MAN: I'm sorry. (*To the audience.*) We all knew.

REWCASTLE: People like your father treated me as though I'd suffered some terrible tragedy. Like death or an incurable disease. They talked in lowered voices and felt embarrassed in my company...

MAN: It was a loss...

REWCASTLE: I'm not so sure it was. She was an emotional woman. Everything was either a tragedy or a triumph to her. Slight blockage in the washing machine and she'd burst into tears. If she found a nice cut of meat at the butchers, she'd run up the stairs singing for joy! You need a steady hand for dentistry... It's not easy to concentrate on an extraction when you're living with someone emotional.

MAN: Flea's fairly calm.

REWCASTLE: She's got to be. To show up her mother. She's never going to be the woman who yelled, 'This house is doomed!' and bunked off to London when the lights fused. My house is quieter without her. Well bless you. (*He raises his glass.*) I wish you every happiness.

MAN: (*Raising his glass, now a little doubtful.*) Thank you very much...
(*The MAN and REWCASTLE go. The OLD MAN is in downstage light.*)

OLD MAN: Lord Byron was drinking too much and his fingers had been bitten by the parrot. His wedding night was spent in a huge bed with red damask curtains, through which the light of the fire and of a solitary taper glimmered. His pistols were ready to hand, owing to his constant fear of assassination, when he awoke and cried out, 'Good God! I am surely in hell!' We were in a small family hotel. In Troutbeck.

(*Light upstage. There is a small electric fire and a stuffed stag's head hanging against a wall. A print of Wordsworth.*)

Which had been the scene of my, I thought, almost immaculate conception. We went into the resident's lounge. Red flock wallpaper. A small electric fire. The moth eaten head of a stag, complete with antlers. A print depicting the poet Wordsworth.

(*The MAN and FLEA enter. FLEA is smoking a cigarette. Carrying a packet of cigarettes and a lighter.*)

MAN: We'd had a slap-up dinner. In the 'Lyrical Ballads – Restaurant Gastronomique'.

OLD MAN: Which we could ill afford.

MAN: And in the resident's lounge...

OLD MAN: Temporarily bereft of residents...

FLEA: They've all gone to bed.

MAN: The residents?

FLEA: They're very old and they've all gone to bed. (*Pause.*) Tell me something.

MAN: What?

FLEA: Why me?

MAN: Why...

FLEA: Why did you pick on me to marry? I knew you were always slightly besotted but....

MAN: I suppose. The element of danger.

FLEA: I was unsafe?

MAN: I never quite knew what you were going to do next.

FLEA: You liked that?

MAN: I liked it...

FLEA: All right then. Let's do it...

(*She goes to the stag, puts her lighted cigarette in its mouth. Starts to unbutton her shirt.*)

MAN: Go to bed?

FLEA: Do it. In the resident's lounge.

MAN: Suppose someone comes in...

FLEA: That's the element of danger... On the floor as near as possible to the electric fire...

(*FLEA lies down beside the electric fire. Starts to take off her clothes.*)

OLD MAN: So Flea called for an act of love.

(*The MAN is on the floor beneath FLEA, also starting to take off clothes.*)

With the moth-eaten stag looking down on us. Her final act of outrage. Her swan song. Not to be repeated. Never to be repeated.

MAN: How do you know?

OLD MAN: Listen to her. Just listen…

FLEA: You know why I chose you? The element of safety.

OLD MAN: (*To the MAN.*) Have you anything to say why sentence of death should not be passed upon you?

(*Light change. Darkness upstage as FLEA and the MAN go. In downstage light, the BOY comes cantering in, riding an imaginary horse as he did in the first scene of the play. The OLD MAN moves to watch him.*)

BOY: Come on, *mes braves!* Scum! Gaolbirds! Heroes of the French Foreign Legion. To the battlements, you rogues and vagabonds! Prop the dead bodies of your fallen comrades in all the embrasures to deceive the crafty Touaregs. The desert rebels on Arab steeds. They'll think we're four times the numbers!

OLD MAN: You're the only boy I'll ever have…

BOY: I am?

OLD MAN: And you're a memory. I can't take you for a walk along the beach.

BOY: Can't you?

OLD MAN: Well, yes. I suppose I can. (*Pause.*) No girls either.

BOY: (*Contemptuous.*) Girls!

OLD MAN: You'll grow used to them. Love them. Fear them, perhaps.

BOY: Honestly! I don't think Beau Geste was afraid of girls.

OLD MAN: Don't be so sure… Anyway, our union was not blessed with issue.

(*Sound of dogs barking.*)

We had the dogs, of course.

BOY: My father…

OLD MAN: Our father. Who possibly now, to his
 amazement, art in heaven...   '
BOY: He wouldn't let me have a puppy.
OLD MAN: Flea made up for it. Three noisy little dogs,
 carefully washed and combed. The hair kept getting into
 their eyes. She treated them like children. (*Pause.*) They
 had an insane affection for me. A passion I could hardly
 reciprocate. When I came home they shot at me like
 bullets from a gun. Wild, with unrequited love. Aiming
 directly at my crotch. I suppose they had a kind of
 courage. They'd bark at anything.
 (*Sound of sea and dogs.*)
 (*Looks out at the sea.*) They barked at the waves of the sea,
 hoping to frighten them off. Which they apparently did,
 retreating at low tide with the terriers paddling out after
 them...
FLEA: (*Calling.*) Heathcliff! D'Arcy! Rochester!
OLD MAN: Flea named them after her favourite characters
 in fiction.
FLEA: (*Calls off stage.*) Come back! All of you. Back to
 Mother, now!
OLD MAN: Those dogs were no cross-Channel swimmers.
 Worse luck...
 (*FLEA enters upstage and calls out to the dogs.*)
FLEA: You're all wet and dirty. We'll get you home and give
 you a nice bath.
 (*The MAN enters, following her on. FLEA goes. The MAN
 stands for a moment watching her go. Offstage song: 'The
 Folks that Live on the Hill'. During this the MAN goes,
 following FLEA.*)
OLD MAN: Time speeds up. That's the trouble. The years
 melt together. It's no sooner summer then it's only thirty
 shopping days to Christmas. The dogs. The *Sentinel.*
 Supper at the Vicarage; Steadily downhill with no
 crossroads, until...
 (*The MAN enters downstage, purposeful and in a hurry.*)
 Sam Brackett, the Editor, wants to see you in his office as
 a matter of urgency.

(*Light upstage. The EDITOR's office. The EDITOR is sitting on his chair. He seems happy. The MAN goes to him.*)

EDITOR: Pottinger!

MAN: You wanted to see me…?

EDITOR: I want to see you on a matter of great importance – to both of us. I've remembered something…

MAN: What exactly?

EDITOR: Those dear old movies we loved so much. *The Editor.* Or *The Detective.* Or *The Leading Star.* Always kept a bottle of this in the top drawer of his desk.
(*He opens the desk drawer, takes out a bottle of Bourbon. Stands, find glasses.*)
You'll take a shot of Jack Daniels won't you, Potty?

MAN: What did you call me?

EDITOR: I called you Potty. Takes less time than Pottinger.

MAN: They called me that at school.

EDITOR: Did they by God? Then we're on the way back… searching for the days of our youth…

OLD MAN: Do you think Sam Brackett, the Editor, could find them – apparently, he hadn't given up hope entirely.

EDITOR: Here's to it, Potty, to youth… Coupled with…sex.
(*He drinks.*)

MAN: What did you say?

OLD MAN: This was not a word we had ever heard Sam, the Editor, utter before.

EDITOR: Drink up, Potty. Not afraid of a shot of bourbon are you?

MAN: Not at all afraid… (*He drinks.*)

EDITOR: Well now. Let me start at the beginning. You know Mrs Elks, our office cleaner…

MAN: Well, of course. She's here every morning…

EDITOR: No longer.

MAN: What…?

EDITOR: Mrs Elks, Dorothy as she has become known to me, will no longer be coming to clean for us each morning at a surprisingly early hour. Mrs Elks, Dorothy…is leaving her work at the *Sentinel.*

MAN: I'm sorry to hear it…

EDITOR: I am not sorry, Potty. Definitely not sorry. In fact, I am overjoyed.

MAN: You mean her cleaning hasn't been up to standard?

EDITOR: Dorothy's cleaning, Potty, is up to the highest professional standards and always has been.

MAN: So why is she leaving?

EDITOR: Think about it, Potty. Did you ever notice Mrs Elks' bosoms?

MAN: Not particularly.

EDITOR: 'Not particularly.' You sadden me, Potty. It's as if you came back from Paris and I said 'Did you notice the Eiffel Tower?' to which you replied, 'Not particularly.' Did you never observe Mrs Elks' bosoms when she plies the Hoover?

MAN: Not in any detail.

EDITOR: They swing, Potty. Her bosoms swing with her movements as she vacuums. Did you never glance at Mrs Elks' buttocks at all?

MAN: I suppose in passing...

EDITOR: I understand. I also was guilty of glancing and passing on. But one day, one recent day, I have to confess I simply stood and stared. She was in the kneeling position, Potty. Adding a remarkable sheen to our corridor lino. Do you know the word 'generous', Potty? Or 'voluptuous', or the phrase 'to die for'?

MAN: Of course.

EDITOR: Then...what can I say?

MAN: So when you noticed Mrs Elks...

OLD MAN: Apparently for the first time...

EDITOR: Up to then, it's no exaggeration to say I regarded my life as wasted. I had to act quickly.

MAN: What did you do, exactly?

OLD MAN: Was there, in your question, a note of envy?

EDITOR: I invited Mrs Elks, Dorothy, to the set menu which they do very reasonably with half a bottle of wine per person thrown in, down at the 'Tumblers Arms' in Wainscote. Dorothy thoroughly enjoyed the meal. And then – what do you think, Potty...

MAN: You took her to the pictures?

OLD MAN: Didn't you want your Editor to have too much pleasure? Another note of envy.

EDITOR: As you know, Potty. I drive a Ford Popular. It's a reliable vehicle. Reasonably cheap to run. Undemanding on petrol and easy to park. But it's not a big vehicle as you know. Hardly what you would call capacious. And Dorothy Elks is not, thank God, a small lady. But she is athletic, Potty. She fits in. And the hour we spent in the National Trust car park by Wainscote woods in my Popular I count among the happiest of my life. Dorothy Elks is a remarkable woman. A very lovely lady. All moist...

MAN: I thought you said you would never allow a woman to touch your underclothes....

EDITOR: Those days are over, Potty. Praise be to God. Those days are over. I live with my unmarried sister, if you remember. A natural tyrant is Noreen. Ordered me about from childhood upwards. When I told her I was about to leave home, she collapsed on the lounge sofa breathless and lost for words. It was very satisfactory.

MAN: Can I just ask one question...?

OLD MAN: Are you looking for a fly in the Editor's ointment?

EDITOR: What is it, Potty? I've got nothing to be ashamed of.

MAN: Is there a Mr Elks?

EDITOR: Went in search of work up to Newcastle-on-Tyne ten years ago. Hasn't been heard of since. We are free, Dorothy and I, to do exactly what we want.

MAN: Which is?

EDITOR: Cruising

MAN: You mean...?

EDITOR: Dorothy's got all the brochures – and there are some remarkable offers. The Caribbean Get Away. Up the Nile to the tombs of the Pharaohs. The Fjord Experience. With Spice Winds to the Malayan Archipelago. I plan to spend the next year, Potty, with the smell of the sea in my nostrils, four star eating available in the saloon and Dorothy Elks available in the starboard bunk. So what I have to tell you, is... (*He stands, points at his chair.*) This chair is now available. (*Pause.*) And you, I would think, are a natural inheritor.

(*Fade to darkness. Party noises.*
Lights upstage. Christmas decorations. Mistletoe. The MAN
appears. He is about to make a speech to the offstage partygoers.)

MAN: Good evening…

(*The noise continues. A voice calls 'Quiet please'. The noise*
subsides.)

As your Chairman, may I wish you all a warm welcome
to Coldsands Newspapers Limited's annual Christmas
party. You will have all heard that we have made a
successful takeover bid for the Shrimpton *Advertiser.*
Which means we have the largest, many would say the
most successful, newspaper organisation on this
particular strip of the East Coast.

(*Applause.*)

We shall continue to deal with local issues with the
fearlessness and sense of balance which marked Sam
Brackett's time at the *Sentinel.*

(*More applause.*)

By the way, you might care to hear this cable which I
have received from Sam. (*He takes a piece of paper out of*
his pocket and reads.) It was sent from the cruise ship SS
'Last of the Pharaohs' and it reads 'well done old cock…'

(*Laughter.*)

Well, we all know Sam. 'You made it to the top. Hope
you enjoy it. The pyramids have got nothing on Dorothy
Elks, now Brackett, so we spent most of the days below
decks b…' I better not read that bit out…

(*Loud laughter.*)

'So. Happy Christmas to you all and enjoy the party…'

(*Applause. 1970s rock music. The MAN goes and returns,*
doing his best to jive with a girl.)

I'm dancing…

OLD MAN: You've put on weight but got lighter on your
feet. Toes in your well polished brogues are twinkling.

MAN: I'm dancing with Elsie Dareham from the picture desk.

OLD MAN: Clutching to youth like a drowning man to a
straw. And being the boss, she allows you to dance her
towards the mistletoe.

(*The GIRL kisses the MAN quickly and walks off to join her friends.*)

Pleased with yourself, are you – now you're Chairman of the board?

MAN: How could I have turned it down?

OLD MAN: Easily. As easily as Mavis escaped.

MAN: Perhaps I didn't want to escape.

OLD MAN: That's what I'm afraid of.

MAN: I'd worked hard for years. Why shouldn't I have taken it?

OLD MAN: The Editor's Chair of the Coldsands *Sentinel*...

MAN: And Chairman. After old Monty Graves died. It wasn't just the *Sentinel*...

OLD MAN: Oh I know. Amalgamated with the Dewfall *Chronicle*, not forgetting the Skimmington *Argus*, the Wildfell *Standard* and the Plashy *Independent*.

MAN: It's all very well for you to talk.

OLD MAN: That's all I can do now. Talk.

MAN: It's all you could ever do. Telling me I was missing my chances. What sort of help was that for God's sake?

OLD MAN: No help. You'd given up before I could do anything for you.

MAN: (*Now angry.*) Given up? I'm Chairman of a decent company. I've got a perfectly respectable income. A good marriage. I've bought the Vicarage and put in reliable central heating...

OLD MAN: Is that what you want on your tombstone... 'He bought the Vicarage and put in reliable central heating'?

MAN: I don't care what's on my tombstone... Anyway – you're always talking about tombstones...

OLD MAN: Ethel Bembridge. Late of this Parish.

MAN: (*Impatient.*) You're always remembering that!

OLD MAN: You've given me so little else to remember.

MAN: That was years ago. It was one night...

OLD MAN: One...totally unexpected night.

MAN: So forget it! I promise you, I have...

OLD MAN: She may still surprise you.

MAN: She was a liar!

OLD MAN: Let's say...a teller of stories...

MAN: More than a little dotty...

OLD MAN: You mean...

MAN: All right. Let's face it. Mad. She ran away...

OLD MAN: Leaving me nothing to look back on – except a world of sanity.

MAN: Oh do stop thinking about yourself! When I'm your age...

OLD MAN: When you get here, I shall be waiting.

MAN: I hope I'll've learned to keep quiet... Not keep on looking backwards. Blaming people. Count our blessings.

OLD MAN: A good marriage.

MAN: We don't fight. We don't throw crockery. Or leave home. We don't cheat...

OLD MAN: Only within the bounds of respectability. Perhaps at the office party...

MAN: That meant absolutely nothing...

OLD MAN: If only.

MAN: What...

OLD MAN: If only it had...

MAN: When I think of what I've managed to make of my life in Coldsands...

OLD MAN: What am I to think? What am I honestly to think?

MAN: I don't think I've done anything to be ashamed of...

OLD MAN: That seems to me...to be a terrible pity...

MAN: And I'll tell you what I haven't done...

OLD MAN: So much...

MAN: I haven't lived my life for the sole purpose of keeping you entertained... In your old age!

(*Light change. The Vicarage. The MAN sits, opens the newspaper. Reads. FLEA comes in with breakfast things on a tray.*)

FLEA: What're you reading? The gardening article?

(*The MAN goes on reading. Doesn't answer. We hear MAVIS' voice off stage.*)

MAVIS: (*Off.*) From our correspondent on the spot. The Telegraph's new trouble shooter – Mavis Whitney.

(*Sound of bullets, shouts,* 'Viva la revolucion!' *A clattering typewriter. MAVIS enters in downstage light.*)

'From my hotel bedroom I can see the angry crowd in the square. They're using sticks, stones, pick-axe handles

– any sort of weapon they can grab in a hurry. There's a hail of bullets, rattling against the wrought iron of my balcony as I type. The young soldiers, some of them look like boys just out of school, seem embarrassed and reluctant to fire on the crowd. Last night, the General granted me a personal interview in his fortified study in the Palazzo Real. He was wearing a silk dressing gown and sipping French champagne. An old man whose days are numbered. "My people," he said, "don't understand democracy. They are children, looking for a father." I felt his aged hand, like a dead and fallen leaf, on my knee...'

(*The MAN can hardly believe it.*)

OLD MAN: Mavis, who was after you at the fete. She'd published a novel.

MAN: I didn't read it...

OLD MAN: Something you'll live to regret. Missing Mavis. So, there she is, clattering the old Remington, looking down at the revolution. I wonder who she's got on the bed?

MAN: A handsome half-caste?

OLD MAN: Possibly. With honey handy.

MAN: I don't want to think about it.

FLEA: What did you say?

MAN: Nothing, darling. Nothing. (*Pause.*) I can't believe it. Mavis Whitney...

FLEA: I seem to remember her. The colourless girl.

MAN: No colour to her eyebrows.

(*A dog barks.*)

FLEA: Shut up, Rochester.

MAN: (*Looking at the papers.*) She doesn't look so colourless. Not in the photograph at the top of the column.

FLEA: Darling...

MAN: Yes, darling?

FLEA: Butter a piece of toast for Rochester, would you?

(*Light fades upstage. In downstage light, the MAN enters pushing his FATHER, very ill, in a wheelchair, wearing pyjamas, his knees covered with a rug.*)

OLD MAN: Three more shopping days to Christmas and our father faced death.

FATHER: I have to tell you honestly. It's a time to be honest.

MAN: You don't have to tell me anything.

OLD MAN: What're you afraid of? Some ghastly sexual revelation? A mistress in Tunbridge Wells? A second family in Hackney? An elderly illegitimate child working in Norwich as a car park person?

MAN: I'm afraid of something like that.

OLD MAN: Nothing you want to hear less than details of our father's sex life.

FATHER: I'm in a state of uncertainty...

MAN: Whether to leave his money to the car park worker?

FATHER: Which to fear most. The existence or non-existence of God?

OLD MAN: Don't say, 'Wait and see.'

MAN: Why don't you...wait and see? (*Pause.*) Our father looks pained.

OLD MAN: I told you...

FATHER: Have I more to fear if there is or isn't a God? Which is worse...? Judgement or a long nothingness? It's a cause for anxiety.

MAN: Why should you fear judgement?

OLD MAN: The risk of a question like that is that he might tell you.

FATHER: I've always steered clear of the law, old boy. Never put a foot inside a law court. I'm not sure I could cope with it. I should fear judgement of any sort.

MAN: He called me 'old boy'. For the first time in my life...

OLD MAN: For the first time in his death.

MAN: Do you think he found himself in the dock? In some celestial version of Coldsands Magistrates' Court?

OLD MAN: I can't tell you that.

MAN: I suppose it won't be long before you find out.
      (*He's going, pushing the FATHER out.*)

OLD MAN: (*Looking after him.*) For a man of your age... You are singularly lacking in tact.
      (*Sound of the sea. The MAN re-enters with the MOTHER. They're walking on the beach together.*)

MOTHER: I'm not staying here.

MAN: What, Mother?

MOTHER: In this old vicarage. I'm certainly not staying...
    Not now your father's gone.

MAN: What're you going to do?

MOTHER: Travel.

MAN: Travel where, in heaven's name?

MOTHER: I wrote to Pansy Pangbourne. I was at school
    with her. We fancy the idea of Morocco. We might take
    in Italy on the way...

MAN: Can you afford it?

MOTHER: Easily. Your father spent nothing. When we've
    travelled enough, I'll settle down with Pansy. In Lamorna
    Cove...

MAN: That'll be exciting.

MOTHER: In Cornwall. We shall do exactly as we like...

MAN: Exactly?

MOTHER: Into the sea at sunrise. Without a stitch on, most
    probably.

OLD MAN: With my father dead, Mother became
    embarrassingly liberated.

MAN: I can't understand it...

MOTHER: We used to do that.

MAN: Who used to...?

MOTHER: Your father and I. Into the sea here, stark naked.
    Before anyone was up.

OLD MAN: You don't want to even think about it.

MOTHER: It was before your father had his doubts.

MAN: (*Incredulous.*) He had faith?

MOTHER: Oh yes. It made him far more lively. In the
    churchyard, for instance.

MAN: What did you do in the churchyard?

OLD MAN: Do you really want to know?

MOTHER: Absolutely none of your business.

OLD MAN: She's right of course. To leave you guessing.
    (*He goes.*)

MOTHER: We shall travel light.

MAN: You and Pansy?

MOTHER: Rucksacks. That sort of thing. We shall take the
    minimum. And we shall get talking to people.

MAN: What sort of people?

MOTHER: We shall fall into conversation.

MAN: Who with?

MOTHER: Anyone. People on buses. Trains. Waiters.
Pansy's particularly good at getting secrets out of
waiters. She's also good at French.

MAN: Will that help…?

MOTHER: They speak French. In the camel market in
Ou'zazat.

MAN: Where's that?

MOTHER: Almost in the Sahara Desert. Pansy's looked it
up and we're aiming for it.

MAN: So…how soon?

MOTHER: Am I going? Almost at once.

MAN: We're going to miss you.

MOTHER: Absolute rubbish. You won't miss me at all.
You've got a wife now. I'm leaving it all to her. You, and
the vicarage…

(*The MOTHER and the MAN go. The OLD MAN enters
with the One-Man-Band. He puts it down, starts to sing and
play it. He sings seven lines from 'Night and Day'.
The BOY enters, angry.*)

BOY: That's mine!

OLD MAN: It was yours. Mine now. Playing it. To
remember how badly we both sang. I told you, I found
it. A dusty and damp one-man-band, shoved away in the
attic. After our mother died and we bought the place
from the Church of England.

BOY: Was my bike there?

OLD MAN: What…?

BOY: My three speed Raleigh… Is it still there?

OLD MAN: It's of no use to us now.

BOY: But is it still there?

OLD MAN: In the loft over the garage. But our bicycling
days are over.

BOY: Why are you playing with my things then?

OLD MAN: What?

BOY: Why are you playing my one-man-band? My best
Christmas present.

OLD MAN: Perhaps... If we could get back to the moment when you unwrapped it.

BOY: I had a good idea what it was – it was what I wanted.

OLD MAN: When you played it for the first time. The very first time. What did you play? Can you remember...?

BOY: 'It Was On the Isle of Capri'. I had the sheet music.

OLD MAN: Let's hear...

(*The BOY sings two lines of 'It Was On the Isle of Capri', drumming as well. The OLD MAN then sings the next two lines. They both laugh.*)

If we could get back to when you played that...

BOY: We just did...

OLD MAN: Not really. We thought about it... But if we could...

BOY: What it...?

OLD MAN: I could tell you how to do everything differently. (*Pause.*)

BOY: I'm sorry, I've got to go.

OLD MAN: No. Don't...!

BOY: I'm taking this with me. Because it's mine.

(*The BOY picks up the One-Man-Band and goes. The OLD MAN moves downstage.*

FLEA enters upstage and starts to lay the table. The MAN enters and sits at the table. The OLD MAN moves towards him and speaks.)

OLD MAN: It's time.

MAN: What?

OLD MAN: Time I took over.

MAN: (*Unbelieving.*) Already?

OLD MAN: Is it sooner than you expected?

MAN: Much sooner.

OLD MAN: It'll go much more quickly from now on. (*Pause.*) Wish me luck.

MAN: (*Getting up.*) Good luck.

OLD MAN: Thank you...

(*The MAN goes. The OLD MAN sits down at the table. FLEA sits with him. They are silent for a while.*)

Flea and I had very little to say to each other. And what we said was not of absorbing interest.

FLEA: More shepherd's pie?

OLD MAN: No, thank you. That was ample.

FLEA: Like your mother made it... Before she walked off into the sunset...

OLD MAN: (*Sadly.*) Exactly... (*Pause.*)

FLEA: When you next put out the rubbish...

OLD MAN: What?

FLEA: Milk cartons go to be recycled, like the newspapers. And bottles do have to be kept separate.

OLD MAN: Flea had taken on the environment. Uneaten shepherd's pie went into a separate bin to save the universe.

FLEA: You remember what I told you about the milk cartons don't you?

OLD MAN: Yes. Of course I remember. (*Pause.*) You don't smoke now of course.

FLEA: You know I don't. Filthy habit!

OLD MAN: And yet there was a time...

FLEA: (*Reluctant.*) When I was very young...

OLD MAN: When you gave a stag's head a cigarette... Do you remember?

FLEA: (*Looks at him, puzzled and a little cross.*) Do try and stop talking nonsense.

(*The OLD MAN picks up a copy of a newspaper and moves downstage. FLEA takes out the plates and goes. Upstage lights dim. The OLD MAN smiles as he looks at the newspapers.*)

OLD MAN: We announced it in the *Sentinel.* 'Famous writer back in Coldsands. The author of *Wine, Roses and Revolutions, Mexican Nights, There Is A World Elsewhere* and other best-sellers, will be back in her home town. Mavis Whitney will be speaking and signing books in the Imperial Hotel.' (*He goes.*)

(*MAVIS appears downstage. Smiling, elegant, smartly dressed. A queue forms in front of her. The BARMAN, REWCASTLE, the GIRL who was dancing at the Christmas party, form a line with books which she signs for them during offstage song: 'We'll Meet Again'.*

MAVIS has now signed for REWCASTLE and the BARMAN who have gone. As the GIRL hands her a book, the OLD MAN enters with a book and stands behind her.)

MAVIS: (*To the GIRL.*) What shall I write?

GIRL: Just your name. If you'd be so kind.

MAVIS: It would be a pleasure.

(*She signs and the GIRL goes. The OLD MAN hands her a book.*)

MAVIS: What shall I write for you?

OLD MAN: You could put... 'To Henry Pottinger. I introduced him to Lord Byron.' (*As Mavis is signing.*) Thank you very much.

MAVIS: (*Handing the book back to him.*) There you are. We could have a drink, perhaps. (*Quiet.*) Why do I always have to issue the invitations?

OLD MAN: Just tell me where...

MAVIS: First floor. Rooms ten and eleven. You're not walking too well. Better go up in the lift... You'll come?

OLD MAN: I'm not going to go on making the same mistake all the rest of my life.

(*MAVIS and the OLD MAN leave in different directions. Upstage light. Sunlight, sound of the sea. The sitting room of MAVIS's suite. A mini-bar, chairs. MAVIS is opening half a bottle of champagne from the minibar. The OLD MAN is with her.*)

MAVIS: Half a bottle of champagne.

OLD MAN: The mini-bar. In my view the only modern invention which has added much to human happiness. (*Laughter.*)

How've you escaped it?

MAVIS: Escaped what?

OLD MAN: Old age.

MAVIS: Don't be ridiculous.

OLD MAN: A woman in her fifties? No, sixty, perhaps. But fair hair only just going grey. Thin. In a black trouser suit with little jewellery. Lines of a long life at the corners of her eyes. I no longer noticed the eyelashes. She twisted the cork, held it to check the first rush of the bubbles and poured neatly, sliding the wine down against the glass. (*With the bottle open MAVIS fills the glasses. They chink glasses and drink.*)

MAVIS: To you...

OLD MAN: To you. Who introduced me to Byron.

(*MAVIS sits, kicks off her shoes as the OLD MAN speaks of what he sees to the audience.*)

She sat down, after all that standing, and kicked off her shoes. She bent forward and felt the tiredness of her feet. Then her hands moved upwards, stroking her legs, appreciating the slimness of them. With a touch of make up on the eyelashes, I thought, she now looks beautiful.

MAVIS: Are you happy?

OLD MAN: Happier...

MAVIS: Than what?

OLD MAN: Than I was. I'm doing a lot to the garden.

MAVIS: Such as...?

OLD MAN: Planting vegetables.

MAVIS: Is that a good thing?

OLD MAN: A very good thing. You're always thinking of the future. Next spring. Next autumn. They've got to be prepared for. And fighting the enemies.

MAVIS: What enemies?

OLD MAN: Slugs, caterpillars, moles, mice, pigeons. Last year the pigeons ate all my peas. Not like your life...

MAVIS: I do still think about you, Henry.

OLD MAN: After two husbands...?

MAVIS: During the husbands. Occasionally... If I have to be honest. And the son.

(*Pause.*)

OLD MAN: The what did you say?

MAVIS: When I left and started work. Doing anything at all around Fleet Street. When I had my little boy.

(*Pause. He looks at her. Wonders*)

OLD MAN: How long after you left?

MAVIS: He's grown up of course. Never married. Innumerable girlfriends...

OLD MAN: How old...?

MAVIS: How old would you like to think he is?

OLD MAN: What do you mean?

MAVIS: What if I said he was born...exactly nine months after I left Coldsands. (*Pause. He looks at her.*)

OLD MAN: And when we met in the churchyard...

MAVIS: Don't worry. You said you kept some... At least three. In your wallet.

OLD MAN: (*Relieved.*) Oh, God! I'm glad you remember.

MAVIS: You'd be surprised. How much I remember.

OLD MAN: So I got out the wallet?

MAVIS: (*Smiles.*) Funny. I don't think I can remember that.

OLD MAN: So it's possible?

MAVIS: The world is full of possibilities…

(*Pause.*)

OLD MAN: Where is he now?

MAVIS: My son?

OLD MAN: What's his name?

MAVIS: Shall we say…Nicholas, Nicky. I call him Nick.

OLD MAN: (*Doubtful.*) Do you really…?

MAVIS: Nick. A sharp single syllable. Of course he's very handsome.

OLD MAN: And he's – where?

MAVIS: Africa. Australia. South America…

OLD MAN: Doing?

MAVIS: Deep sea diving. Breeding horses. Making a movie. Helping starving people.

(*Pause.*)

OLD MAN: Why don't you tell me the truth?

MAVIS: I want him to be… Whatever you would have liked most. And I know what that is.

OLD MAN: What exactly?

MAVIS: Yourself. Yourself, if you'd done what you really wanted.

OLD MAN: So. He's just like those other stories you invented…

MAVIS: Not exactly like those…

OLD MAN: Not exactly? Why?

MAVIS: Well. It was true wasn't it. We were together in the churchyard.

OLD MAN: (*Smiles.*) And we're here together now.

MAVIS: So we are!

OLD MAN: And all the years between?

MAVIS: They can be. Whatever we think of them.

(*Pause.*)

OLD MAN: I understand…

MAVIS: Do you?

OLD MAN: You're here to sell a work of fiction.

MAVIS: And to see you again. I hoped I'd see you again, Henry.

OLD MAN: Well then. Here we are. (*He moves, looks out at the sea.*) The windows were open and the sea was glittering. The door was open to her bedroom and I saw the satin covered king sized and, beyond it, the marble bathroom with glass shelves on which various fragrances and toiletries were set out for guests to steal. I had no choice but to make a suggestion. (*Pause.*) Would you mind if I kept my socks on?

MAVIS: When?

OLD MAN: Making what I'd be prepared to call love.

MAVIS: No...

OLD MAN: No, you don't mind if I keep my socks on?

MAVIS: No, we're not going to make love.

OLD MAN: 'The great object of life is sensation – to feel we exist. It's this aching void which drives us to intemperate but keenly felt pursuits.' You know who said that?

MAVIS: Yes, I know... We missed the bus...

OLD MAN: I've missed you.

MAVIS: Let's say... I moved on.

OLD MAN: You don't mind my asking?

MAVIS: I'd have been quite offended if you hadn't.

OLD MAN: But you said no?

MAVIS: That's what I said. (*Pause.*) Don't worry because there'll be plenty more buses coming along, I don't think you should miss any of them. (*Pause.*) I'm sure it's very exciting planting vegetables, but...

OLD MAN: But?

MAVIS: I told you. The world is full of possibilities.

OLD MAN: For me?

MAVIS: For all of us.

OLD MAN: There's so little time.

MAVIS: Then make the most of it.

OLD MAN: Catch the bus?

MAVIS: To somewhere. (*She kisses him.*) Goodbye Henry. (*The hotel room darkens. MAVIS goes into the darkness. The OLD MAN moves to downstage light. Sound of the sea. The OLD MAN watches and the MAN enters.*)

MAN: Is this where it ends?

OLD MAN: It ends for you here. Yes.

MAN: And for you –

OLD MAN: Not...quite yet.

MAN: This is all it is?

OLD MAN: You had your moments. Remember them...

MAN: And you?

OLD MAN: I remember them too.

(*The BOY appears.*)

BOY: What're you doing?

OLD MAN: I'm not about to pinch the tops out of the broad beans.

BOY: Why not?

OLD MAN: I have got to go somewhere.

BOY: Where?

OLD MAN: Catch a bus.

BOY: To Skimmington?

OLD MAN: Perhaps, further than that. (*To the MAN.*) Where did *he* go?

MAN: Who?

OLD MAN: Lord B. Of course. Rattling in his coach with his doctor and his mistress and his dog Boatswain. Down the dusty road to Brussels and Geneva, Pisa and Venice, Ravenna and Missalonghi. Last stop Missalonghi.

(*He goes upstage, where he picks up a suitcase.*)

MAN: What's going to happen to us?

OLD MAN: You'll stay here. In the garden of the house where you lived. (*He looks at the BOY.*) You're the only boy I've ever had.

BOY: Come on *mes braves!* Desert scum! Beloved gaol birds. Heroes of the French Foreign Legion.

MAN: Ethel Bembridge, widow, late of this parish.

OLD MAN: Goodbye.

(*The light dies on the MAN and the BOY. Light on the OLD MAN as he leaves upstage, carrying his suitcase.*)

The End